Girl, WHAT you gonna DO with your MONEY?

To Camilla,
What a blessing
it is to know you. Thank you
for your love & support.
Mega Blessings!

ALSO BY TI'JUANA GHOLSON

Girl, WHAT you gonna DO with your MONEY? Teen

Girl, WHAT you gonna DO with your MONEY? Children

You are loved

TI'JUANA GHOLSON

Girl, WHAT you gonna DO with your MONEY?

A Business Woman's View on Why

Money Matters for Women

REVISED EDITION

MAX Publishing

VIRGINIA

Published by MAX Publishing, LLC

Published in the United States of America.

ISBN- 13: 978-1-970097-00-9

Disclaimer/Warning:

This book is intended for lecture and educational purposes only.

This program provides no guarantees of effectiveness for ALL Persons. This book is the opinion and experience of the writer and serves as a guide to support the lecture or training offered by the writer and team.

Book cover illustrations (front and back) by Trevor Lucas, Anomaly Art Studio

A change of the mind will change a life.

TAG

This Book's Purpose

This book is intended for the woman who wants financial confidence with the ultimate goal of financial freedom. She is your everyday woman who works hard and has ideas on the inside that could bring her the cash flow she desires. She may also have had to make a shift in life due to unforeseen situations, to keep up with industry changes or to shift from a national crisis.

This is the "typical woman":

- A wife, mother, executive, relative, friend and/or colleague
- The "Girl Next Door"
- The woman who is fed up with her current situation
- The woman who wants to enhance what she is already doing
- This woman could own a busines OR aspire to do so

Dedication

I dedicate this book to my favorite daughter, Ti'Mari Lawren-Antjuanette (inside joke) and future granddaughters. I want a blueprint left for you to know that you can do whatever you set your heart to. YOU come from good stock and YOU have the goods. YOU were born with what it takes, so go forth and DO great things!

To my mother, my new angel who has taken her place in another realm, Valerie Y. Tucker... Mommy I MISS you like nothing I have EVER experienced before! To my granny, Mary who I have watched make a dollar out of fifteen cents, I Love you Foxy Lady... we are in this thing together! And to my mother-in-love Glenda, thank you for your consistent love and support always. You are the greatest in my eyes!

To my sisters, nieces, goddaughters, cousins, clients, and mentees: YOU can do this! If I can... so can YOU!

To my sister-friends, aka the Sistahood Divas, you are always in my corner, encouraging me to be ME and pushing me to be better. I thank you for that! You ladies are TRUE friends that I call FAMILY!

To my business colleagues, my networking group Ladies Impacting Professional Systems (AKA L.I.P.S.™), YOU inspire me! Let's keep making money moves!

And lastly but NOT least… To my LOVE, Mr. Gholson, the man who is always cheering for me and pushing me to be great. Thank you for allowing me to share parts of our story with the world! My Love, you are an AMAZING man! I am so honored to share life with you! What an amazing journey we have been blessed to explore and enjoy together. God could not have chosen a better person for me to pour my love into than you. I love you with all my heart and I honor you with the purest of heart.

Let's continue this journey of forever… Always!

Why Money *Really* Matters for Women

Women and men accumulate wealth differently: Women have an unfair disadvantage from BIRTH!

By simply being born a woman, women have an unfair disadvantage when it comes to wealth accumulation.

 Women are historically seen as the "homemakers", automatically causing them to not be taken as seriously as men in the workplace. According to the US Census Bureau and the Labor Department, in 2016 women earned 80 cents for each dollar a man earned.[1] Due to lower wages, females were historically automatically behind the wealth curve.

Ladies, if we are not able to pay for our day-to-day expenses with what we bring home, then saving money doesn't seem like a realistic option. And for some, the reality is there is nothing left to save. This reality also leaves women more vulnerable to unexpected life changes compared to men. Situations such as divorce, single parenting, accidents, injury, illness, or death of a spouse can cause a drastic turn towards financial hardship.

---

[1] Donnelly, G. (2017 September 13). The Gender Pay Gap Narrowed in 2016. But Only by 2 Cents. Retrieved 13 September 2018, from http://fortune.com/2017/09/13/gender-pay-gap-2016/.

A REAL-LIFE EXAMPLE:

One of my closest friends was doing well in a management position at a major corporation. She was reportedly making more money than she ever had, close to $50,000 annually (still below a male's average salary). Although her salary was decent, it did not leave much room for saving.

Did you know the average recommended savings plan for household expenses is a minimum of six months to a year of living expenses in case of an emergency?

I can assuredly tell you that my friend did not have anywhere near that amount saved. Most people I know do not.

Suddenly, my friend was stricken with an unforeseen illness which caused her to not be able to work full-time. She was forced to work part-time until her health eventually required her to take medical leave. Things were stable for a while, as long as her sick leave covered her extended medical leave of absence. But when her health situation never returned to normal or improved, concerns arose.

My friend was left with a decision to make that would change her financial health forever. Should she ignore the doctor's orders because she needed to work and make money, or should she ride it out and hope her job would allow her to use some sort of disability benefit? Well, LIFE decided for her.

As her health continued to decline, her medical leave and savings also declined until both were depleted. To make matters worse, the doctor ordered her to stop working. What was she supposed to do?

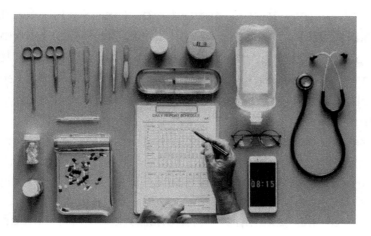

Officially unable to meet her daily expenses, not to mention her expensive medical care needs, her employer fired her.

In the majority of states, your ability to no longer fulfill your job obligations as described, is legal grounds for termination. Some states are at-will states meaning your employer can terminate you at any time without a reason.

✍ **What would you do in this situation?** ✍

_____

_____

_____

Naturally, my friend turned to the Social Security Administration to apply for disability benefits. However, the process is not that easy and often requires legal counsel. Those who are approved are often denied benefits at least once and the process can be lengthy. So, in the meantime, what was she supposed to do? In addition to her failing health, my friend lost pretty much ALL she had. She ended up selling her possessions and moving in with her parents, still with no income.

This real-life example demonstrates the danger of financial insecurity and the vulnerable position many women are in. If you are living paycheck to paycheck today, an unexpected circumstance can make it impossible to survive. So what is a woman to do? How do we navigate our current society, knowing that we are behind the wealth curve just because of the gender we were born with?

How do we earn the money we not only deserve but work so hard for? There are multiple ways to achieve this and I will share them with you throughout this book. That leads me to one question for you...

Girl, WHAT you gonna DO with *your* MONEY?

Introduction

What's MONEY Got to do with it?

Exploring your feelings and renewing your mind about money.

- *Money is not everything*
- *It's not about the money*
- *Money doesn't grow on trees*
- *Money is evil*
- *We can't do it because we don't have enough MONEY!*

And the list goes on and on. Many of us have heard the same or similar phrases from those that raised us or from the media. Many of these phrases have taken residence in our minds and have become beliefs we have accepted over time.

Money, regardless of how important or unimportant one might say it is, controls our world. How? The amount of money you possess determines where you live, the type of car you drive, the clothes you wear, the food you eat, the activities you participate in and so forth. Money may not be everything, but the lack thereof can be everything!

As a life and business coach, my primary focus with my clients includes evaluating and discussing their plans for wealth (present and future). We start with a chat discussing their "vision" which leads to goal-setting. However, before we can discuss goal setting, we must discuss the elephant in the room... the current state of their money!

This is one of the hardest client conversations to have because emotions are flared, and realities must be faced that the client is often not prepared for. We must discuss what the client was told in childhood regarding money and the impact those voices have today. One of the biggest challenges my clients face is the acceptance of what momma, grandma, pops, uncle, or auntie told them may no longer be good for *their* financial life.

Then we must uncover the truth about their credit and spending habits, by reviewing their credit report and savings history. But before we can move forward with any of these details and get down to business, we first must discuss how the client *feels* about money. Yes, I said how the client *feels* about money. Although this occurs in the beginning of our relationship, it can only happen if the client wishes to progress.

Ti'Juana, why would your client not want to progress? Isn't that why they hired you—to HELP them in the first place? Although that sounds simple enough and is true, **money** is a sensitive topic for many. Like me many did not grow up being educated in money matters. Money is often a taboo topic that many are ignorant in and most do not seek help in this area until they are deep in debt. The sad part about operating in this mindset is that so much could have been done prior to a person losing control of their finances.

Here is one of the key reasons that money matters for women:

Money, and the use thereof, often comes
with an emotional attachment.

When I ask a client how he/she *feels* about money, often deep emotions surface and for some those emotions are accompanied by tears. I have witnessed clients working with me to establish substantial savings, spend it all or give it to family members who may have placed them in financial distress in the first place. So how can you prevent your emotions from hindering your wealth?

First, be honest and acknowledge that money is an important part of your life. No guilt, no shame; it is not sinful or selfish for money to be important to you. Second, acknowledge that nothing gets accomplished in the world without money. Third, examine your beliefs about money by writing them down and challenging yourself. Ask yourself:

Do I believe what I was told about money?
Is that belief WORKING for me?

If you believe what you were told about money and its working for you, keep it! If not, throw it out! It is as simple as that. But if you never take the time to quiet yourself and explore your feelings about money, you may find yourself constantly struggling with money regardless of the level of success you achieve.

A REAL-LIFE EXAMPLE:

B renda is a lady who grew up in the "hood" or what may be referred to as the "ghetto". Put it this way, the neighborhood she was raised in, offered limited housing choices or opportunities for the low income. There was never a surplus of money in Brenda's household. Money was so scarce that it was not present enough to be discussed. This caused Brenda to fixate on what it would be like to have money and wealth. Her main motivation at times *was* money.

Every get-rich-quick scheme that came along would find Brenda in the front of the line to take advantage of it. Money excited her and she was all in. She would talk about how much money she could make with each scheme. However, after a few months without the quick results she desired, the ideas fizzled just as quick or until the next get-rich-quick scheme came along.

Brenda carried the same mindsets into her employment. Each time someone told her that she could make money doing this or that or she could make more money if she lived in this or that state, Brenda ran in that direction. "I'm moving to such and such state because you can make a lot of money there." Or "I'm moving to such and such state because my family member can help me get a good government job with benefits." Brenda did this for many years until she was exhausted.

Finally, one day, Brenda landed a business. One of her friends sat her down and said, "Hey, I got an idea that works for me and I want to share it with you. Are you in?"

Of course, Brenda was in. After all, she had said yes to every other money scheme that came her way. This would be no different. And, since it was recommended by a trusted friend, what did she have to lose? Brenda started the business and did well. She made a lot of money quickly. That money looked and felt good to her. She had never had that much money in her bank account at one time in all her life! Well, except for maybe tax season and maybe not even then.

Oh, Brenda made a lot of money but, with that money, she made a lot of poor decisions. She began to buy things that she did not need and on a frequent basis. She began giving her money away just as quick as she earned it, whether to family members or so-called investment ideas that came along. She justified those ideas by reasoning that she was "creating other streams of income". She tried several new ideas, but, just like her prior get-rich-quick schemes, they all failed.

Once again, Brenda found herself in financial trouble. Even after making a lot of money, she found herself struggling with her thoughts about money. These emotionally led thoughts dictated her actions.

Do you understand what just happened here? I am going to repeat a few key details to ensure that you understand the lesson.

Brenda made more money in her business venture than she EVER had in her ENTIRE life. The financial flow she received was four times greater than she ever received working for someone else.

The more money Brenda made, the hungrier she became, resulting in her not making the best decisions. In fact, because she made so much money, she reasoned she should take the money and "flip it." Are you starting to see a pattern here? Although Brenda experienced some level of financial success, she did not change her mindset of a poor mentality. She was not able to truly handle the money that she was making in her seemingly prosperous business. Her childhood experience of the lack of money and never having enough embedded fear in Brenda, causing difficulty in her creating real wealth.

Brenda finally mastered how to *make* money, but now she needed to master how to *keep* it. The money went out as quickly as it came in with little going to savings. Brenda had no more discipline with making money than she did when she lived in income-based housing and was poor. Without a mindset change, Brenda did not progress past where she was before.

Key Points:

➤ Exploring your feelings about money is essential in order to make a mindset change.

➤ Making more money does not guarantee financial success.

➤ Once mastering how to MAKE money, one must master how to KEEP it.

So, I ask you again...

Girl, WHAT you gonna DO with *your* MONEY?

Table of Contents

Common Excuses/Barriers Blocking Wealth

In your life, do any of the following sound familiar?

- ➢ I don't make enough money
- ➢ I'm in debt
- ➢ I don't manage money well
- ➢ I'm a shopper!

As an employer, I've discovered that:

Regardless of HOW much money a person makes, if he/she does not know how to manage it, he/she will end up BROKE!

People do what they want to do and pay for what they want to pay. I love to hear a woman say to me, "I don't have enough money to save" and I can visibly see the amount of money she *could* have saved based on her appearance. She sashays in designer clothes/shoes, manicured nails, pedicured feet, and expensive hairstyles. I often find an excess $100 per month in the average woman's budget just by evaluating her shopping habits. Now there are always exceptions to every rule. The woman that does not shop for designer clothes may spend lavishly in other areas or have an outrageous cell phone plan where she could save a few dollars if she monitored more closely.

The point *is,* unless you are dirt poor or have absolutely NO money coming in, we ALL could find excess money IF we tried.

A REAL-LIFE EXAMPLE:

One of my fashion-conscious friends loves to shop. She *must* have the latest this and that. She has a passion for those shoes with the "red bottoms" and has a closet FULL of them. She often brags about her having a "designer shoe closet." To her credit, she works as an executive at a major corporation, earning at least a six-figure salary, with travel perks, a company card, allowance and all the fringe benefits. BUT, although this friend has a six-figure salary on paper, she does not have a six-figure saving or investment plan.

From her outward appearance–the expensive designer clothes and all the accessories, luxury cars and jet-setting life you would think she would have a massive savings and investment plan. Well, I am here to tell you, her savings are no greater than my friend in the previous example who lost her job due to her failing health.

We discuss her lack of savings periodically when she brings it up and talk about starting her dream business and being financially independent. However, as the years go by, this conversation becomes nothing more than that... just a conversation. So, what is the hold-up? How can she be no further along than someone who makes at least half her salary and with none of those fringe benefits?

KEY MONEY BLOCKERS:

appropriation

Appropriation

APPROPRIATION!

Are you reading this and saying, "Ti'Juana, you reading my mail? How did you know?"

Or are you saying, "Yes, this is me; HELP!"

27 Girl WHAT!

Well, I can give you one tip that you can implement right now to change the trajectory of your financial health. However, it comes with the following disclaimer: *You are not going to like it, but it does WORK!*

Are you ready to know what it is?

But first I ask you...

Girl, WHAT you gonna DO with *your* MONEY?

Key Points:

➢ We all could find access money if we tried.

➢ Looking successful does not equate to being successful.

➢ Appropriation is important in managing money.

Two Dirty Words that Unblock Poverty

Delayed Gratification

W hat a harsh thought to some.

What do you mean I have to wait?

But I want what I want NOW!

This is typically the response I get when people ask me how I acquired the financial freedom I have now. I explain that I had to wait for some things. I had to use what I had, save, and simply wait.

Most people do not want to wait because we live in a society of *right now*. Credit makes it so easy for us to buy now and pay later. Living our lives this way puts us at financial risk. God forbid, we end up like my friend and lose our job. And then our world shatters.

You see, if I can just get my six-figure friend to delay buying expensive shoes and save just one of her paychecks every month, I could show her the road to financial freedom. It does not take much, and with her and her husband's hefty salaries, she can AFFORD to save. But the question is, will she delay her wants for her future?

Will YOU delay your wants for your future?

✍ **What are your *must-haves*?** ✍

_____   _____

_____   _____

_____   _____

_____   _____

✍ **What do you feel when you hear "delayed gratification"?** ✍

_____

_____

_____

_____

✍ **Go back to your list of *must-haves*. For each item,**

describe what you would gain if it were delayed. ✍

Must Haves	_Benefit of Delay_
_____	_____
_____	_____
_____	_____
_____	_____
_____	_____
_____	_____

After reviewing your results, what changes are needed to make for a better future?

✍ **Needed Changes:** ✍

_____

_____

_____

_____

_____

_____

_____

_____

_____

_____

_____

_____

_____

If I Knew Then what I Know Now

I take nothing away from my journey. I know what I know now because I did not have a clear picture growing up which challenged me to study money matters for myself.

I had a small view of the example my grandmother showed me by at least writing bills down. However, that was the extent of it.

Mind you, my grandmother did not sit me down and show me HOW to manage money. I learned by being *nosey* and *snooping* around. My grandmother used to leave a list of bills written in a notebook on the kitchen table. This was her form of record keeping and showing Papa what the household expenses were. I was an inquisitive kid, so I PEEPED in the notebook! :o) Today I am glad I did because I learned that at a minimum you need to know WHAT you owe for a clear picture of where you are financially. Thanks Granny!

I also, in a non-traditional way, learned from my mother how to save money by bulk shopping. That lady used to put toilet paper on layaway to assure that we had what we needed. And today I thank her for it. I chuckle about it, but my mother's toilet paper layaway method taught me how to lessen my trips to the market and keep more of my money in my pocket for saving. However again, there were no formal conversations about saving money, what to do with it and where to allocate it to make it grow however, I picked up a few tips from their examples.

Because I did not have perfect examples of how to properly save and accumulate wealth, it forced me to be proactive and conduct research. My personal interest of how money works and my desire for financial education led to an unrivaled literacy that changed my wealth potential, which I will share throughout this book.

✍ **What were you taught about finances in childhood?** ✍

_____

_____

_____

_____

✍ **How did that impact your financial habits?** ✍

_____

_____

_____

Key Points:

➢ Delayed gratification is saving now and buying later.

➢ You need to know what you owe for a clearer picture of your financial situation.

➢ Financial education/literacy can change your wealth potential.

✍ **Record any additional thoughts regarding your financial freedom?** ✍

_____

_____

_____

_____

_____

_____

_____

_____

_____

_____

_____

_____

_____

_____

_____

3

The Root of My Success

I know, I know. You would love for me to share my list of secrets and tips with you right now and send you on your way. While I would LOVE to do that, doing so would only cheat you and lead to failure. Here is the truth:

Wealth, like success, is a journey and everyone has his/her own road – as well as idea of sUccess.

My keys to sUccess (no, the U is not a typo), are far more varied than the discussion of money. As a female and owner of multiple businesses, I have learned a few lifelong lessons over the years that have helped me achieve my personal level of what success is to me.

I have made mistakes along the way, TOO MANY to mention. I am no different than you or the next women. I have shopped too much, overspent, put the desires of others before my own, not saved enough and splurged on whatever I wanted and when I wanted. However, there came a time when I was tired of living the same way and getting the same results. When you get sick and tired of being sick and tired, you will make a change.

I decided that enough was enough and that if I never purchased another shirt, a pair of jeans, a tube of lipstick or a pair of shoes, I would LIVE!

FAILURES

Like most, I have failed at staying focused on a goal and saving money. But the small voice on the inside of me never allowed me to settle. I never had the desire to simply give up.

MOMENTS OF REGRET

The only regret that I have is that I did not start my journey to financial freedom earlier. There are a few things I could have put in place 30 years ago, but I was stuck in survival mode at that point in my life. I was a young wife and mother, and my focus at that time was assuring that my family simply ate and were properly housed and clothed. But TODAY is a new day and I am a firm believer that time is redeemed for those who never give up!

I kept going, I did not stop. I gave myself no other option but to be successful. My success was important to me and my "why" was to change my legacy. My family history has been rewritten, shifted, and changed for the better. Hope has been restored and renewed. A sense of pride has been birthed and there was no way I could do anything but succeed. You can make the decision from this day forward to do the same.

✍ **What is your WHY/reason for success?** ✍

_____

_____

_____

_____

_____

Tee... Tee Baby, Tee-Tee is what they called me

A s a young person, I knew there was a better life that I could live. I felt deep down in my heart that there was more. Although I grew up in a modest environment, it was not as horrible as some. I just knew that there was more.

As the years passed, I was exposed to other races and cultures, proving better lifestyles existed. Do not get me wrong, I am grateful for my life and my upbringing, I just always had a desire to have more. Some may call me different–in fact, they did, but I just simply KNEW there was a better life I could live.

Television

Television and music were my main outlets as a young person. They exposed me to the world and allowed me to see pictures of what I was feeling in my heart. Although there were not many programs that depicted black people in the 70's and 80's, there were opportunities to see how people lived. And many of the TV characters lived the life that my heart yearned for.

Instead of simply admiring the lifestyles of the characters, I asked the question HOW... HOW can I live like that? And from that point forward, I believed my journey to financial freedom began. YES, I trace my desire for financial freedom to childhood.

✍ **Who is your success role model? Why?** ✍

_____

_____

_____

_____

✍ **What are the secrets of his/her success?** ✍

_____

_____

_____

✍ **How do you plan to achieve his/her level of success?** ✍

_____

_____

_____

_____

You see, being able to see yourself doing better and being better is the first step to changing your situation. And I am not necessarily speaking of being able to see with your natural eye, I am talking about seeing with your heart.

Some would call it an activation of your faith. I say it is *knowing* that you cannot be shaken, no matter what. And when you can see something in the physical form, it's simply a confirmation of what your heart already knows.

I was also blessed, for a short time, to live and go to school in another country. I was blessed to experience another culture and see life from another side of the world, from a different perspective. My first experience on an airplane was during childhood, which again sparked the desire to want more and propelled me to ask the question *why*?

As a teenager, I begin to grow into my "self". I was quirky, weird and had my own opinions. I began to recognize what I wanted and how I wanted to believe. I continued to carry that mentality of "there's got to be something better" and I began to carry myself as such.

BOY did I get flack for that! It was NOT accepted in my community to have thoughts and beliefs different from the masses. I mean "who do you think you are?"; "you trying to act white" and "you live in a fantasy world" were just a few of the comments I had to endure.

✍ **Have you shared your success goals?**

What has been the response? ✍

_____

_____

_____

_____

✍ **How have these responses impacted your mindset?** ✍

_____

_____

_____

_____

I could not even dress differently without being criticized. That was the time in my life that I learned that being different, or having your own beliefs, was NOT accepted. There was no place for opinion and there damn sure was no place for a girl like me to think more highly of herself than she should.

As I am writing and reflecting on it now, I get tickled because I had no clue that I *was not* supposed to dream. In one breath I was told I could be whatever I wanted to be. In that same breath, I was condemned for thinking differently than the masses. Why couldn't I just sit down and be "normal"?

I believed so strongly that my life should be better than it was at the time, that I would clean, scrub, straighten and make my mother's home to look the way I thought *we* should live. My mom, being a single mother, had no issues with me being the neat freak teenager I was. Mom was too tired to keep up with housework or stop to pay attention to the details that haunted *me*. So, she was simply fine with me picking up the slack.

When I reflect on those days, I can pinpoint the root of my attitude of always wanting more. Always wanting something better and always believing that there was a better life I could live. From a young age, I dared to dream, and I practiced that lifestyle in my mother's home. I saw further than my situation at that time. Again, I, little small town girl had the audacity to dream! I dreamed in silence and I staged a comfortable place for me to dream–RIGHT IN MY MOTHER'S HOUSE!

Key Points:

- ➢ Knowing your WHY is important in your journey of sUccess.

- ➢ Dreaming allows you to see pass your current situation.

- ➢ Success goals helps one to stay focus; a success role model gives a view of what *could* be.

✍ **Did you give yourself a place to dream? If so, what did you dream your life would be?** ✍

_____

_____

_____

_____

_____

_____

_____

_____

_____

_____

_____

_____

✍ Can you pinpoint your first desire for financial freedom? ✍

_____

_____

_____

_____

_____

_____

_____

_____

_____

_____

_____

_____

4

How my First Love Introduced me to My First Love

What a joy it was to meet my first love, Lawrence, in 1985. I was 14 and he was 15. We met through a mutual friend that we call family. At that time, we were phone buddies because I was not permitted to have a "boyfriend" at that age.

Lawrence and I had so much fun together, right over the phone, but we lost contact when his family moved, and his phone number changed. Back in those days, a move sometimes meant a telephone number change. You know, way back when the house phone was all you had. :o)

We lost contact and found each other again at a church function, somewhere around the Spring of my 16th year. I remember this vividly because he asked me out to his ring dance only a month after we started dating. Yep, when we reconnected I could "officially" date then. It was during this season that Lawrence meant that he was NOT going to lose me again. I mean the brother set his stake in the ground for me and sealed it with a poem that I still tear up today just thinking about it.

I bring up my longtime boyfriend because he validated my dreams. He was very easy to talk to and I would talk, talk and talk to him about how I wanted to live my life, how successful I wanted to be and how I had my little life all planned out. He would listen and dream with me.

This is when I first felt that I was not crazy and that I could attain my dreams and what television showed me. And guess what? I had one believer, my Lawrence! I could NOW conquer the world!

 Lawrence and I fell in love at an early age. We could not get enough of each other. We became "the couple" in our family and amongst our friends. You did not see one without the other. I mean, I had his name on my car's license plates. We created the joint names way before the celebrities started merging their names together. We were *Tee & Lon* and we were going to name our daughter Ta'Lon. Lovers for LIFE, point blank PERIOD!

We were so bad that if one were without the other, people would automatically ask, "Where's Tee or Lonnie"? Yeah, it was pretty serious! We were such a couple that our parents were comfortable with our relationship. We blended into each other's families like we were one family. The children of the families looked up to us and we were trusted with the EVERYBODY's children. We became involuntary "mentors", which is how we received practice for our future children.

It was BEAUTIFUL! We had a sweet high school love affair until off to college he went! I thought I had lost my best friend. We missed each other so much that he would make his way home every weekend to see me. Not much for a college experience, right?

He would even show up at my high school during the weekdays and convince a guidance counselor to allow him into my locker to leave me surprises. I was the envy of all the girls. "Aww, Lonnie is so sweet", they said. "You're sooooo lucky!"

He even bought a ring and proposed to me at 18! I suppose he did not want to lose me while he was off at college. I foolishly said yes because I loved him, right? And having a real diamond ring at 18 was exciting! I STILL own that ring!

Well, we were so in love that I followed him to college instead of going to my first choice. It was during that first year of college that my life would change and change forever.

Key Points:

➢ Find someone to dream with.

➢ Find someone who gets you.

➢ Choose LOVE!

5

Life Happens but it Doesn't have to Stop Your Success

L'Antonio TaiQuan Gholson is what we called him. At that time, Lawrence did not want a junior so, like many of us back then, we made a combination name. We gave that bouncing 6-pound, 11-ounce little boy a combination of his daddy's first and middle name and a middle name that would be similar to his mommy. We called him by his middle name.

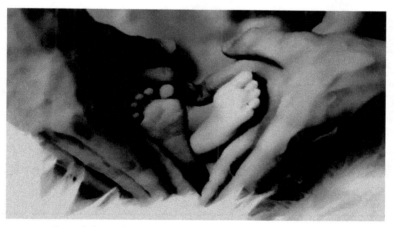

He was the life changer... God's dream for us, right? Riiiiiight! Becoming a mommy TOTALLY changed me. I became a CRAZY person! Not only were my dreams of having that good life even MORE important, but now I HAD to make them work. I had a little person depending on me and "he didn't ask to be here." That was my mantra at the time.

✍ **What life changes have impacted your success?** ✍

_____   _____

_____   _____

_____   _____

_____   _____

✍ **How have you adjusted? Have you lost momentum, pressed on, or just gave up?** ✍

_____

_____

_____

_____

✍ **What support do you need? Have you asked for it?** ✍

_____

_____

_____

_____

I put so much pressure on Lawrence. I can now look back at that time and say, *WHEW, I am lucky he stayed with me.* There were moments when I simply lost my mind! But we BOTH had dreams that included each other, and my Lawrence was the perfect gentleman, not to mention the perfect father for our son!

The first year was a whirlwind. We were still attempting to "do the right thing" by pursuing the "American dream" of getting a college education. But this time we had to do it with a child.

Our village stepped in and helped. Thank God for my grandmother who watched our son for a deeply discounted rate, aka FREE, so that I could go back to college. BUT college looked a little different this time around.

First of all, I had to come home and go to the local college. Secondly, I had to juggle a college schedule with a baby. And Lawrence, just like any man and rightfully so, was looking for attention as well as trying to achieve *his* college degree. We decided to attend the same college again, only this time closer to home.

You should have seen us. One would walk out of class and one would walk in handing the baby carriage to the exiting one. We called little TaiQuan our "college baby" because there were a few occasions that he had to attend class with us due to schedule conflicts. Boy was this a challenging time! Challenging but doable. The dreams were even stronger in my heart. Remember, there was no room for giving up–this baby "didn't ask to be here." As time went by so did our frustration. Lawrence decided that he needed to make more money than the part-time job he had at the hospital. He had to take care of his new baby.

So, he made the decision to drop out of college and get a full-time job. Some may think that this was not the best decision however it was the best decision for *us*. I will save that story for another book, but Lawrence felt he needed to do something and for HIS son, so he did. I fell in love with him all over again!

Throughout the years, we have had our ups and downs like any other couple, especially since we started out so young. There was the transition of living together while young, being broke and trying to figure out life. A lot of things did not go according to plan and certain life events seemed to add to the stress of it all. Did I forget to tell you that one year and seven months after the birth of our son, we welcomed little Miss Ti'Mari Lawren-Antjuanette Gholson? Yeah, another combo name.

Things sometimes were tight, and we wondered where were those dreams of living a better life? I also had to learn how to be an independent woman, a wife AND a mother. Life hit us hard! Although Lawrence had a job and

I was in school, there NEVER seemed to be enough money. Lawrence then began to plot our exit strategy.

Unbeknownst to me, he had a serious life conversation with an older cousin about the benefits of going into the military. He then proceeded to speak with several recruiters before choosing the US Army. After weighing all his options, he came home to break the news to me. Then came THE proposal (the second one). His proposal went a little something like THIS:

> "I went to talk with a recruiter today and I've decided to go into the military. He said that I can make more money if we get married before I go in."

And I said, "You're not leaving ME in Petersburg by myself with two kids." So, the wedding planning began. We proceeded to get married quickly as basic training was awaiting Lawrence's arrival. By this time, I was 21 and Lawrence was 22. Yes, it took us two years after our son was born to get married.

Unlike many in my family, I refused to allow anyone to convince me that I needed to get married JUST because I was expecting a baby. I did not wish to lie to my children and pretend that they were conceived in marriage and then have to live up to that lie for the rest of my life.

✍ **TRUTH: Do you feel like your family has forced you to put your dreams on hold? How so?** ✍

_____

_____

_____

_____

_____

_____

_____

✍ **What are your deal breakers (or no's)?** ✍

_____ _____

_____ _____

_____ _____

_____ _____

_____ _____

_____ _____

_____ _____

The New York Experience

Although I will save some of this for a future book, I could not talk about why money matters for women without sharing with you the New York experience. Lawrence's first duty station, (remember he was in the military), was in upstate New York. As his wife and proud mother of two, I was all too happy to follow my husband.

Happy until I quickly found out that we would not be getting military housing as soon as we thought. We ended up staying in a military hotel for about three to four months, cramped with two small children. Oh sure, the young naïve me thought it was sexy at first, even exciting until the number of days increased and so did our lack of money and comfortability.

Do you know how costly it is to live in New York as a young couple with now, two young children and very little money? There was only so much entertaining I could do with the kids in a small hotel room. And the snow there was unbearable! I had to find a job! I HAD to have my own money. And what type of wife would I be if I allowed my new husband to foot the bill alone? I HAD to help-out (or so I thought). What I KNEW I had to do was get out of that hotel room!

As the wife of a new, military serviceman, I had limited time with my husband. He HAD to go to work and I felt as if I did not have a life. He had a life, or so it appeared compared to mine. He had an outlet at work and could have adult conversations. And there I was, alone in a hotel all day with two babies. GooGoo, GaGa, was not much of a conversation if you catch my drift, but it was enough to make me scream. I needed a life. I needed a job.

But how many of you know that finding a job was not easy, especially in the 90's. To make matters worse, we were in a small town that was not used to black people. Finding a job took so long that I decided to go back to school instead.

Once in school, I found a part-time job in the evening. And that is when the reality of being a working mother suddenly hit me. I was not ready to allow my children to go off with strangers. Although I was a young mother, I was very, very, VERY picky about the way I wanted to live my life. And leaving my kids with strangers was not in the plans.

Eventually, I got it together, because I knew that my life had to be better and at that time, a college education was one of the ways I thought would make it better. One of the reasons that Lawrence dropped out of college and joined the military was so we could have military housing while I completed school. The plan was for me to finish school first, and him complete his first military term after which it would be his turn to return to school. We were a team, and the end goal was to have a better life.

Reflecting on those times proved one valuable lesson for me regarding money matters:

One can still be on the journey of sUccess,
even if life throws a few curve balls and
things do not go exactly as planned.

My husband's enlisted pay would not allow us to remain in the hotel for a long duration. When we *did* find a quaint, little place for our family, it was on top of an elderly couple's home and it was kind of creepy at night. But at least we were somewhere that we could halfway afford, and the family could stay together. We were still on the pathway to success; it was just a little deterred from the initial plans due to us having children quicker than we thought. Nevertheless, we had love, we had our children and we had each other!

✍ **What are the blessings you have despite the curveball's life has thrown you?** ✍

_____

_____

_____

_____

_____

✍ **Did you notice that the blessings outweigh the curveballs? Explain** ✍

_____

_____

_____

_____

_____

Key Points:

➢ For every dream there is a sacrifice.

➢ Everything does not always go as planned.

➢ There are blessings despite curveballs thrown in life!

✍ **Record any additional thoughts regarding your life experiences that have brought you to the place you are now financially?** ✍

_____

_____

_____

_____

_____

_____

_____

_____

_____

_____

_____

_____

_____

_____

_____

6
Why do Women Business Owners Earn Less Money than men?

Women business owners often earn less than men for various reasons. Sometimes the type of business a woman chooses causes the gender pay gap. For example, a daycare owner may make less than an IT consulting firm. Another issue is often a lack of exposure or connections. If no one knows who you are or that your business exists, you may not be able to compete with an influential male business owner who may effectively market.

Often women feel intimated when networking with men.

Here is another major issue that I find with women entrepreneurs: Women often feel intimidated when networking with men. That is why I have created a local networking group so that women business owners can come together and support each other.

Unlike our male counterparts, women often struggle with confidence. Many women do not even take the steps to business ownership because of fear of failure. I coach and talk with women all the time, almost PUSHING them through the door of entrepreneurship. They have what it takes but second guess themselves because of societal "norms" – (i.e., You must have a degree in this or a certification in that). Too often we second guess ourselves out of success.

✍ **What are the reasons you think women business owners earn less than male business owners?** ✍

_____

_____

_____

_____

_____

_____

_____

_____

_____

_____

_____

_____

A REAL-LIFE EXAMPLE:

I am reminded of a particular client that I met with weekly to discuss her business goals and aspirations. She appeared to have some sort of a plan for what she wanted to accomplish, but she never took any steps towards her vision. I would ask her week after week what she was waiting for and she would come up with every excuse she could think of:

- "It isn't the right time."
- "I'm not sure what town I want to start my business in."
- "I don't have enough money."

(Does any of these excuses sound familiar? Be honest.)

I remember one day we went through our regular salutations, pulled out her goals and began our discussion. Apparently, this was the day my client got tired of coming up with excuses and looked at me and said: "I'll tell you the truth. The reason I haven't started my business is because of FEAR".

Fear is no laughing matter. Fear can stagnate a dream, determine one's actions and even dictate what one believes. Fear preys upon one's belief of what he or she is capable of. When I find fear present in my coaching clients, I must address the root cause before we can move forward.

In the above example, my client did change her belief and finally started her business, but I had to almost PUSH her through the door. It took a lot of effort to get her to the place where she believed in herself.

✍ **What are some of your fears of starting a business?** ✍

_____

_____

_____

_____

_____

_____

_____

_____

Can women have it all?

One question I am often asked (and one that you probably have asked yourself) is: **Can women have it all?**

My answer? Sure, you can, but not ALL at the same time! Using myself as an example, motherhood alone is difficult, so adding a business to it takes some serious pre-planning. It is doable yet you must have a strategic plan. What worked for me in the initial stages was to involve my entire family in the business, from office tasks (our children were professional paper shredders and filers), to housework, to planning our family activities. The family was involved. Although difficult at times, it was imperative to simply stop and just do family! After all, isn't part of being a business owner having freedom to spend time with family?

I often respond that the reason I went into business for myself was to have extra time with my family. I was buying my freedom. However, there were times when it became extremely difficult to do so with the demands of a business start-up.

Key Points:

➤ Sometimes the type of business a woman chooses causes a gender pay gap.

➤ Fear of failure causes stagnation.

➤ Woman can have it all if it is planned.

✍ **Record ways that you can balance family time as you seek financial freedom.** ✍

_____

_____

_____

_____

_____

_____

_____

_____

_____

_____

_____

7

Discovering your Wealth

As we all know, there are several ways to acquire wealth. However, two common ways are to: earn more money and reduce your spending. Over the next few pages, I will give you a few strategies for both.

Before you start, be honest with yourself about your current financial situation. Many can tell you how much money they make and what is earned after taxes. But few can honestly tell you what they owe.

This may make you feel uncomfortable or be a subject you would rather not talk about, but you will need to change your mindset if you want to discover wealth and have financial freedom. You cannot fix what you refuse to address.

Free yourself from the guilt and shame. The decisions you have made up to this point are behind you. We are starting with a clean slate and starting over. To do that, you must be willing to face this subject head on and get the financial help you need.

The worse person to lie to is yourself.

Reality Check:

Although that unique pair of shoes or outfit that catches your eye says, "buy me", I assure you that it is NOT a need. If you are going to increase your wealth and pursue financial freedom, there are some sacrifices that must be made, regardless of your income.

✍ **Create a list of luxuries (spending choices) that you usually spend money on (i.e., manicures, entertainment, etc.? ✍**

_____

_____

_____

_____

_____

_____

_____

_____

_____

_____

Here is a checklist of spending choices that can be eliminated, either temporarily or permanently, until your financial/saving's goal(s) are met:

Don't		Do
Nail Salon		Do It Yourself
Hair Salon		Do It Yourself
Retail Therapy		Shop in your own closet; use accessories to change your look/ outfit
Cellphone		Switch to pre-paid services
Fast Food		Cook at home
Entertainment		Rent movies for $1 or $2
Cable		Switch to Hulu or the like
Drive unnecessarily		Carpool, walk or bike ride
Use Credits Cards		Layaway, Thrift Shops or Consignment
Impulse and Unplanned Spending		Use coupons, discount shop and plan using weekly store ads

I want you to really think of how you could use the above list to immediately increase your current income. In addition to that, consider the following as ways to earn additional money. Now that the world has experienced a Pandemic it is no longer difficult to put these and other creative practices in place nor SEE yourself following these simple money earning/saving techniques on the next page.

Ways to Earn Additional Income

Closet Sell:

Sell all clothes, shoes, jewelry, purses, household goods, gifts, etc. that you do not use or want anymore. Sell using an online platform like Poshmark.

Offer Ride-Sharing Services:

Earn $ with your car giving rides or delivering food and other items.

Side Hustles:

People pay for convenience. Research something that people want and offer it. Find a need and fill it (my husband calls it the FINAFI principle).

Brand Ambassadors:

Some companies will pay you to promote their brand.

Part-Time Job:

Maybe work from home or at your favorite store.

Ask for a Raise:

Know your worth. Ask for the raise!

Rent Your Extra Space

Freelance:

The Pandemic has brought much creativity out of many. Discover your inner creativity and create yourself a money-making opportunity.

The Root of It All

How are you feeling about the eliminations and additional ways to earn income? Are you finding it hard to let go?

✍ **Write your thoughts below:** ✍

_____

_____

_____

_____

_____

The problem is often what we have been taught about money from our childhood. Women are rarely taught to develop a relationship with bankers and to view them as partners versus a scary entity when you need a loan.

Many women are not taught to be financially savvy and learn about investments, savings, and retirement strategies. Women are taught to take a less aggressive role in pursuing financial freedom than men. As a result, the pay gender gap exists regardless of whether a woman is an employee or a business owner.

The following checklist is a beginner's guide to money management for women.

	Checklist for Money Management
☐	Review your Credit Score
☐	Know your Debt-to-Income Ratio
☐	Pay down your debts
☐	Check your interest rates
☐	Know your spending habits
☐	Establish an emergency fund
☐	Establish a retirement plan
☐	Know your retirement figure & date
☐	Check your insurance premiums

Money Management Checklist

- ➤ **Review your credit score annually.** Take advantage of printing your free credit report each year.

- ➤ **Know your debt-to-income ratio (and reduce it as much as possible).** Start by writing down what you bring in and what is going out.

- ➤ **Pay down your debts.** Plan and devise a strategy to pay your debts down regularly until they are paid in full. Take one debt at a time.

- ➤ **Check your interest rates.** Regularly check your interest rates and negotiate with creditors to reduce rates whenever possible.

- ➤ **Know your spending habits.** Keep track of what you spend by writing it down and saving receipts. At the end of each day/week add your expenditures. Look at your receipts to see what you spend the most money on.

- ➤ **Establish an emergency fund.** The standard is at least 6 to 12 months of your wages in your savings account for emergencies.

- ➤ **Establish a retirement plan.** If you work for someone, take advantage of any offered retirement plans that works for you. Be faithful to the plan and you will see it add up over time. If you own a business create your exit strategy. Many business owners do not think establish a retirement plan. This is even more important when you do not work for someone else.

- ➤ **Know your retirement figure and date.** Whether employed or self-employed, you need to know how much money is necessary for you to retire at the age you want to retire. Once you know that figure, you can devise a plan to create the cashflow that will take care of you when you are no longer able to actively work or run your business.

- ➤ **Check your insurance premiums.** Many Americans are either underinsured or over-insured. Make sure that you regularly check your insurance policies for adequate coverage and the right price.

A couple other tips:

- ➤ **Learn about the investment market.** Google information to educate self. Attend free classes at your bank.
- ➤ **Take advantage of free money.** If you work for someone check to see if the company offer a company match for each dollar you invest (or a specified amount)? Take advantage of it.

✍ **Add other money management tips you have learned along the way?** ✍

_____

_____

_____

_____

_____

_____

_____

Key Points:

- ➤ Two common ways to increase wealth is to earn more money and reduce spending.

- ➤ You must change your mindset to discover wealth.

- ➤ Some sacrifices must be made on the road to financial freedom.

8

A Mindset Change

Some of you are saying by now, "Okay Ti'Juana, I've followed you through seven chapters of this book and I'm not sure if you've told me ANYTHING that I either didn't already know or haven't heard somewhere before. You have not listed any steps to HOW I can reach my financial goals, fund my dream(s), fund my business... NOTHING! You have not given me the *formula* to my financial success! WHAT is IT?"

Well, I will say this—what you are asking for is simple yet complicated. It is a conversation that starts with your mindset. The question is *how do YOU feel about money*? What I have discussed in the previous chapters are only a few areas that must be addressed. And you are right– many of the pointers I shared are familiar. But my question to you is, although you have heard them before, have you practiced the listed suggestions? If so, how are they working for you? If not... WHY? WHY haven't you practiced them?

From my experience, and from what I have seen in my practice, most of my clients THINK that they are ready to make money and start a business to do so. However, when we get to the heart of their dreams and goals, money is something that many are the most uncomfortable with. The root of this uncomfortableness often is related to what they were or were not told about finances as a child (like me). For others, the source of the uncomfortableness is what they have learned along the way from society or ideas they have created in their own minds. As a result, I spend a great deal of time discussing finances with my clients.

All the steps and goal setting will not override a limited mindset. Before you can achieve your ultimate goals of success, business ownership, financial freedom and everything that goes with it, you must first peel back the layers of the mindset you have formed up to this point.

You will achieve what you believe, including your subconscious beliefs.

So, I ask again, **WHY haven't YOU practiced what you have heard before?**

As I have previously described, I grew up in humble beginnings, not knowing much about money. As I have built my businesses and wealth over the past 20 years, I have learned that most people are just like I was. Most have not taken the time to educate themselves on finances, neither have they faced their financial realities. Most have either inherited or picked up their financial mindset along the way and have accepted what was given to them.

I am encouraging you to break free! Break free from those old mindsets if they no longer suit you. Break free from what you were previously told if it no longer serves your financial goals. I know, I know, this will be one of the hardest steps to take because it requires you to admit that what you were taught is all wrong!

………… Breathe!........................BREATHE!........

Okay, let me say it this way: What you have been taught about finances and wealth is all wrong... for YOU! Admit that mama's, grandma's, and auntie's ways do not serve the life that YOU desire to live. Once you admit that, you must decide if you really want to do what it takes to move you towards your dreams.

This, my friend, is the point of self-actualization. Here you will have to face your own truths and really look at where YOU stand financially. This is not something anyone can do for you... this is all on YOU!

Girl, WHAT you gonna DO with your MONEY?

✍ **List the practices you have tried in the past to help your financial situation.** ✍

_____

_____

_____

_____

✍ **List the practices that have worked.** ✍

_____

_____

_____

_____

✍ **List the practices that have NOT worked.** ✍

_____

_____

_____

And you want to know the secrets/steps to success, right? For me, it is as simple as 1-2-3: seeing, believing and DOING. Sound familiar?

STEP 1: SEE

Some refer to it as faith, others call it hope. The ability to see something when there is nothing to see is the first step to changing your financial situation.

Remember, as a little girl, I used television as my muse to see what I did not see around me. Then I closed my eyes and dreamed. I dreamed dreams of the lifestyle I wanted to live. I challenged what I saw around me every day and asked the question, *how can I live like those I saw on television?* I knew in my heart that there was more, so television was the confirmation that what I saw with my heart was real for me. It could not be shaken!

I encourage you today to give yourself permission to dream. Take time out of each day to close your eyes, see with your heart and see yourself where you want to be. See yourself **financially free**!

Key Points:

➢ See yourself where you want to be.

➢ Seeing with your heart is a knowing that cannot be shaken.

➢ Seeing something in the physical form is simply a confirmation of what your heart already knows.

DREAM!

81 Girl WHAT!

STEP 2: BELIEVE

Seeing *IS* believing right? At least that's what the cliché' says. Naaaaaaah!! Nothing could be further from the truth.

Most people do not believe in themselves as much as they believe in others or what they say they believe. Even if they can see it, they may not believe that THEY can do it, achieve it or receive it.

In my television example, I saw AND I believed. I believed that what I saw on TV was not only good for the actors but good for me too. Most people only see and admire others, but have a hard time believing those achievements are possible for them. What they see and what they believe are in conflict.

I have spent many days trying to convince certain clients that THEY are great, and THEY can do it. They would often compliment me on my accomplishments, but not believing that the same was possible for them. Even after I *show them* tax records, share our obstacles and winning strategies, and then help them to devise *their* plan, they *still* have difficulties believing. If our struggles were identical, some would still refuse to believe for themselves.

> *Seeing is not believing if you do not believe in yourself.*

Breaking that mindset is truly a chore because it requires me to help my clients' revisit their pasts and discuss what they have been told about themselves as well as what they tell *themselves* about themselves. I challenge my clients to acknowledge the voices in their head and challenge those scripts that were played to them or imposed on them (i.e., *"you're not good enough"*). I then challenge them to challenge their beliefs and change the scripts.

Again, this is one of the hardest exercises because, once again, we may have to admit that what we were told by the people we love and that love us, may NOT be good for the life WE wish to live.

Key Points:

➤ Believing that YOU can is half the battle.

➤ Seeing is NOT believing if you do not believe in yourself.

➤ Sometimes what you see and what you believe are in conflict.

STEP 3: DO

It's not enough to see and believe, one must take **action**. Seeing is a part of the battle and believing in yourself is another, but the game changer is when you get up and DO something about your life/your situation/your finances. Only action brings about change in your life!

The television inspiration and belief in what I desired did not change my life or situation. It was not until I put a plan in place and executed that plan that I experienced change. I often hear people say knowledge is power, however, I like to say the application of knowledge is power. I could have seen myself in a better position and even believed that I could do better but, without taking action, there would be no change. By taking action–educating myself, getting my finances in order, starting a business, and working towards my goals of financial freedom–I created MY sense of financial freedom and the better life I envisioned.

Do not stop at seeing and believing... make sure you get to *DOING*. I did, and now I live the life I want to live daily because I took the steps to DO what was needed for the desired end results.

Key Points:

➢ Seeing and believing is not enough if you do not DO!

➢ You must DO something to change your financial situation.

➢ The application of knowledge is power.

86 Girl WHAT!

9

Money Discipline-How to SAVE

"I don't have enough money to save"!

"There's no money left over"!

Excuses—we all have them and we've all heard these statements before. But what are YOU going to do: continue to complain about your money or do something about it?

One of the first places I start with my clients is taking a realistic look at their income and spending habits. We discuss what their expense account looks like or whether they have one to begin with. We review the two parts of the average household expense account: the income (what is coming in) and the expenses (what is going out).

We discuss everything, including salary and other income streams (child support, side hustles, etc.). Then we discuss the daunting side of the expense account: the actual expenses!

Many of my clients do not wish to discuss what is really going on with their money. However, we cannot get to the root of their money issues if we do not discuss what is going out! To increase your wealth, financial goals or have financial freedom, you must be able to have a transparent discussion about your MONEY.

So, what is an expense account? Some refer to this as a budget; I call it an expense account. In its simplest form, an expense account is what money comes in and what money goes out however many do not pay attention to those details (especially the going out portion). Expenses are items such as rent or mortgage, utilities, car notes, loans, supplies, gas and insurance. Extras are items such as hair, nails, makeup, cell phone plans and clothing. Trust me, ladies, it is in these extras that I find the extra hundreds of dollars that clients could use to save. Wouldn't you know that this is the area where I get the most resistance?

What are you saying Ti'Juana? You want me to live a substantially lower level of life than I do now by not having the luxuries I am used to?

Absolutely not! What I am saying is if you wish to fund your dream, birth your vision, and live the financially free life YOU desire, then the practice of *delayed gratification* and *saving* must be your greatest priority.

How do I put this into practice? Again, think of a few practical steps YOU can take to help increase your finances. Review the list from chapter seven. Remember, these are temporary delays until your savings goals are met. Remind yourself that you have a vision to birth and a dream to fund! Financial freedom is your goal!

✍ **What are 3 ways you can save additional money from the money you currently have coming in?** ✍

_____

_____

_____

A REAL-LIFE EXAMPLE:

Corinne was a young woman in her mid-to-late 30s who desired to start a business one day. The problem was she did not have the money to do so and neither did her friends or family members. She did not have the credit to be able to walk in a financial institution and be approved for a bank loan. She did not have any credit cards or money saved at the time of our meeting. What she did have was this big dream and a big desire to start a business and succeed.

Her first questions to me were:

- How do I fund my dream?
- How do I get the money to make my vision come alive?

- How do I do this with the little money I currently have?

My questions to her were:

- What do you do with your money now?
- Have you made steps to save anything to fund your own dream?
- Have you set realistic financial goals?

You see, my philosophy is that you must first believe enough in your own vision before you can motivate anyone else to. You also should be the first to put your money where your vision is. YOU must always be your biggest supporter!

Another key lesson I teach my clients is you first must bring something to the table to attract others. When people see that you are serious, they are more likely to take you seriously.

So, after we weeded through the what's and how's, I designed a savings plan for Corinne. First, we looked at her expense account. She did not have one, so I helped her create a blueprint. We looked at all her expenses (what was going out) and compared them with her income (what she was bringing in). We then looked at her credit report to get a full picture of what her true debt was.

> If you have a large amount of bad debt, that
> should be addressed prior to saving.

Remember, before I move forward with any business owner or client, I always tackle what is going on in their personal finances first. I believe that if you cannot handle the little money that you have now, you are going to have difficulties handling large sums of money!

After discussing her finances thoroughly, we found money in many areas. We looked at her spending habits with eating out, cocktails, loaning money to friends and family and buying hair products. She enjoyed spending her money in these areas and the thought of giving that up was somewhat difficult. Together, we devised a plan.

First, we set aside a small portion of her income as *her* money. This is "fun" money where she can spend it on whatever she wants without judgment. While it is not the amount she was accustomed to spending, it was enough built-in support to keep her from falling back into old habits. Remember, when you are funding your dream, it requires SAVING!

So now that Corinne's "fun" money was set aside, we could focus on the amount of money needed to fund the dream. We looked at all the excess money she spent weekly on eating out, cocktails, hair products, etc. Once we marveled at the amount of money she was spending in those areas, I had her to make a commitment to save that amount. I also had her commit to setting up a separate bank account to put that extra money into. (Out of sight, out of mind.) We agreed that within a six-month period, she should have a specified amount saved.

As the months went by, Corinne began to see the money and got excited. "It was more money than I have ever experienced having at one time", she reported. In six months, she managed to save a few thousand dollars. YES, you read correctly, a few THOUSAND dollars. So now she should be on her way, right? She should be closer to funding her dream and creating a life of financial freedom.

I am sad to report that Corinne spent all the money! Little bit by little bit, dollar by dollar, she found new uses for it by buying clothes, shoes, giving it to friends and family, while forgetting her ultimate goal of funding her vision. It was heart wrenching BUT good to see at the same time. Why?

If this lesson needed to be learned, it is best to learn it in the beginning stages. In this case, she learned this valuable lesson before her business started. Imagine starting your business and having thousands of dollars in the bank that must be used to pay staff, contractor invoices and business overhead expenses frivolously spent. Imagine the embarrassment that would bring. Now imagine the greater impact if Corrine learned this lesson AFTER starting a business. Do you see why I said it was heart wrenching, but good to see all at the same time?

Remember, it is important to tackle your money mindset so that you will not lose everything when attempting to fund your dream. After Corrine depleted her savings, I spent time with her discussing what happened. I asked her what she felt about what she had done and why did she feel the need to spend all that money in opposition to her goals? She honestly said, "Because I wasn't used to all of the money that was there." Having all that money excited her and she wanted to spend it, regardless of the goals she set for herself.

Now you see why we must analyze our basic feelings and emotions about money before we can even get to saving money? Well, because of her spending the initial savings, we readjusted and set new goals for her. We put in a cushion where she could spend just a little bit more "fun" money and we placed stronger restraints on her bank accounts. This time, she was not able to touch the money without going through a banker first, who was going to contact me personally for the final approval.

NOTE: Your bank can set up mechanisms in which you cannot touch your savings until a certain timeframe, (i.e., Christmas savings clubs). This method may help a person that has a hard time saving. Having two sets of eyes on Corrine's bank account not only helped her successfully save the second time around, but it also helped her form a relationship with the banker that did not exist before. NOTE: It is vital to establish a good relationship with a good banker!

Create an Expense Account for Yourself

Income		Expenses		Remaining
$	-	$	=	$
	-		=	
	-		=	
	-		=	
	-		=	

Key Points:

➢ You must know how you feel about money before you can successfully save it!

➢ If you cannot handle the money you have now, it will be difficult to handle large sums later.

➢ It is vital to establish a good relationship with a banker.

10

Getting it Together

Getting it together can be one of the hardest things we can do regarding our money. First, we must take a realistic snapshot of what our money is actually doing *for* or *to* us. Another step I encourage my clients to take is Face the Beast... your credit report!

You would be surprised how many people do not know or care to know their credit score OR are afraid to look at it. I challenge my clients to face themselves and pull their credit report. It is difficult to move forward with your money goals and not know your money status, your credit rating, who you owe and what is really coming in and going out every month.

As a business coach, I find that many of my clientele are interested in small business loans or home ownership yet are afraid to move forward due to bad credit. The irony of that fear is that they often refuse to face the infamous credit report but when they finally do face it, most of the time the report is not as bad as they think. Most can be repaired with a little TLC. But first things first: Pull the credit report! Print it! Face the BEAST!

After printing the report, do not just look at it and then put it down. Adopt a mindset change. Take the credit report, put it in a binder and highlight any areas of concern. Look at the dates and see how long each debt has been negligent. Some debts may be old enough to fall off the report and others may need immediate attention. If you never print your credit report, you cannot devise a plan for repair.

Once the report is pulled and printed, I encourage my clients to take another look at their money and decide what they can realistically pay. Attempt to contact the creditors to arrange a payment plan or payoff agreements/settlements. I encourage them to tackle one debt at a time, one debt per month. Before they know it, the debts are paid off in a matter of months.

When my clients follow the steps, it works! By facing their fears and having an honest picture of their credit and debts, they can create a plan for repair and future success. My clients break through barriers that they have allowed to stand in the way of their dreams of financial freedom. The same can be true for you but, first, you must...

... pull the report!

✍ **What are your fears or apprehensions with checking your credit score?** ✍

_____

_____

_____

A REAL-LIFE EXAMPLE:

Tanya answered one of my social media calls to action and attended my financial roundtable a few years ago. I made myself very vulnerable in that session. I shared more than most business coaches do by opening my life and financial status to those in attendance.

There were approximately 10 ladies in the room; 10 ladies hungry for direction on "how to best use their money." I offered them a peek into my taxes to prove that I made the money I said and to validate my business knowledge. After getting through the preliminaries, I conducted a series of exercises with them regarding how they felt about money. I placed $10,000 worth of cash on the table and I asked everybody how they felt about having that money out there.

Some people thought it was fake; one person jokingly said she hoped it would be a gift later and some people thought it was a test of honesty. I also encouraged them to go around the table and explain why they attended the roundtable and what they desired to get from our discussion. I had them complete a questionnaire. The session turned out to be very enlightening and much more than I expected. Many emotions were expressed, and many tears shed. All in the name of MONEY!

Tanya was so motivated after the day's events, so much so that she decided to take the steps to face her credit report. In fact, she pulled it right there, on the spot, during the roundtable. Once Tanya pulled her report, she learned that she had numerous items on there. Some items were old debts, and some were recently acquired debts. She took my suggestion, sat down, and created an expense account. She figured out how much she could pay her creditors and still survive. After she looked at her money in a realistic manner, Tanya called her creditors and set up installment agreements and payoffs. She did exactly what I said, attacking one debt per month. Before she knew it, her credit score was rising.

In about six months, Tanya's credit situation had turned around: not only did her credit score increase, but some of her old debt fell off. Can you imagine the confidence that Tanya had regarding her finances at that time? She called me and reported her good news with excitement in her voice. She thanked me and cried. She said, "Thank you for making me take the brave step to just look at my credit report!"

✍ **Pull your credit report. Write the date you pulled the report below.** ✍

Credit Report Agency   **Date Pulled:**

_____ **Experian** _____   _____

_____ **Equifax** _____   _____

_____ **Transunion** _____   _____

There are three major credit reporting agencies that you receive your credit report from: Experian, Equifax and Transunion.

You can get all three reports for free each year at www.annualcreditreport.com.

There are also secondary companies that you can retrieve your report from. One most commonly used is is www.creditkarma.com. On this site, you can check your credit score in real time via app or email. [Note: the scores on these secondary sites may be a number or two off in comparison to the major sites, but it gives you general information and allows you to have your credit score at your fingertips 24 hours a day.]

Credit card companies also offer a free listing of FICO scores–the score that creditors use to rate your creditworthiness. If this option is available to you, it would not hurt to review it every now and then.

Face the beast... PULL YOUR CREDIT REPORT!

Girl, WHAT you Gonna DO with YOUR money?

Key Points:

➤ It is important to pull your credit report and know where you stand!

➤ You can get all 3 credit reports for free each year.

➤ Credit card companies offer free listing of your FICO score.

✍ **After reviewing your credit report how did you feel?** ✍

_____

_____

_____

_____

_____

_____

_____

_____

_____

_____

11

Financial Freedom... What is it to ME?

Y definitions of financial freedom:

- Not having to work (unless I want to) and my living expenses are STILL paid.

- Making money while I sleep.

- Having the amount of money, I desire and that makes me feel secure.

- Having control of my time.

That is *my* definition of financial freedom: your desired financial freedom may be an entirely different list.

I am often asked, "HOW did YOU achieve your success?" First, I had to see myself financially free, believe that I could be financially free and then do something to make that happen such as putting a realistic plan in place. My plan helped me to achieve that freedom. Remember, I was not born into money, so I had to seek inspiration, and, from that inspiration, it allowed me to see myself successful. I had to dream that I could achieve the successes and financial freedoms I enjoy today.

In my research and self-education, I found numerous ways to achieve financial freedom and will share a few common ways at the end of this chapter. I found success in creating streams of cash flow that will continue to flow even if I do not show up for work. They will continue to flow even after I am gone, and my surviving family can continue the process if they so desire. You will have to find what works for you and what fits naturally with your lifestyle.

Some of the ways I have achieved financial freedom are owning multiple businesses, business partnerships, real estate investments, intellectual property, and traditional investments such as insurance, mutual funds, and IRAs. I believe in conservative systems that require educating yourself, disciplining yourself and doing something to get you to *your* place of financial freedom.

Q: *Would that really work for me?*

A: Well, that is up to you! You must discover your "why." Why do YOU want financial freedom? What does that look like for YOU and what purpose does it have in YOUR life?

I have learned over the years that financial freedom is not the goal for everybody and that is okay! However, if you are the person that wants to make money "while you sleep", then financial freedom may be a goal that you are aspiring to reach.

For me, coming from a family where I did not have any examples of people living a life that was "financially free", it was initially difficult to sell the idea of financial freedom to others. I remember when I went into business in my 20s, I appeared *foolish* to many! People thought I was crazy and asked, "Why would you leave that good job with those benefits to take a chance on a dream? Why would you go to school all those years, get your college degree and make a decision like that?!"

You see, in our society, the *majority mindset* says to strive for the "American Dream". You are encouraged to finish high school, go to college, get that dream job and work for 30 plus years, retire and get your gold watch (used to be a retirement gift back in the day), so you can live happily ever after in the retirement system. If that is your dream fine, but I just knew that was not the life for me. Again, just by looking at television, I knew there was a vastly different life out there that I could live, I just needed to know *how* so I could do the work.

Today I am glad that I did not listen to those voices. My dreams have come true and then some! I am at a great place in life right now, but I still have a long way to go. I tell people that I am my biggest competitor, because every time I achieve one goal, something inside of me strives to set another! As crazy and as unreal as it may seem, anything that you can dream is **attainable**!

If the dream was put inside of YOU… it is FOR YOU!

No matter WHAT comes your way or what circumstances arise. It does not matter if it is an emergency, pandemic epidemic, economic crisis, natural disaster… WHATEVER! If it is meant to be it WILL be!

RECAP:

There are several practical ways for you to create cash flow streams if you were not born into wealth, including:

- ➤ Business Investments
- ➤ Business Partnerships
- ➤ Real Estate Investing
- ➤ Intellectual Properties (IP): writing books, royalties, owning patents and trademarks
- ➤ Investing in commodities (natural resources such as gas and oil)
- ➤ And more...

*Do your research and find what works for you. Follow YOUR dream to financial freedom!

✍ **Write down your WHY. Why do YOU wish to have financial freedom?** ✍

_____

_____

_____

_____

_____

✍ **Write 3 ways you see yourself achieving financial freedom.** ✍

_____

_____

_____

✍ **Write a list of people who can help you achieve the above.** ✍

_____

_____

_____

_____

_____

_____

_____

_____

Self-Reflection - SEE

✍ **Take time with yourself. Take time to SEE. Meditate and write your plan of action. HOW will *you* achieve financial freedom (step by step)?** ✍

_____

_____

_____

_____

_____

_____

Key Points:

➤ The goal of financial freedom is individualized!

➤ Explore *why* you want financial freedom. What is your "WHY"?

➤ Financial freedom is not everybody's goal and that is ok.

12

Educate Yourself!

Let's back up for a moment. In my many discussions with women regarding finances, I often find that although many quickly throw their hands up and say, "I'm not good with money", they are often the bookkeepers, the negotiators and the bill payers of the family. From the savviest saver–the woman that has the ability to "make a dollar outta fifteen cents"–to the mindless shopaholic... women often manage the finances of the home.

So why is it that women feel they are no good with money? From my personal observation, it is due to a lack of financial education. One of the greatest downfalls I have noticed in our school systems is the lack of financial education. This was true when I went to school as well as what is being taught today. Many people, not just women, are simply not educated in the subject of money.

I encourage women to educate yourselves. As you are facing your beliefs around money, take the time to counter them with financial literacy. I know you may be thinking like some of my clients, *"where do I start"?* Or *"I can't possibly understand what I'm reading"*. But I encourage you to start small with books like this one (and thank you for choosing mine).

Pick up pamphlets from your bank. Sit down and talk with your banker. Build relationships with financial professionals. Building relationships are important and people love to share their expertise with others. Find out if there are any financial classes being taught at your bank or credit union. Who knows, you may even discover that your bank offers FREE seminars at many of their local branches?

Google financial terms and just allow your mind to expand regarding money. If you continue at it, one day the terms and wording will become less intimidating and more familiar. Very soon you will be more comfortable in simple conversations about money. It amazes me that the area that many struggles with the most is still considered a taboo topic. The feeling that "we should already know" often hinders us from learning more.

Remember, we are women: we *thrive* off getting our questions answered and getting things done! So, I encourage you, my friend, to treat the subject of money like we treat anything else and ASK QUESTIONS!

You CAN DO IT! Get it done!

YOU ROCK!

Girl, WHAT you Gonna DO with YOUR money?

Key Points:

➢ Women are often the bookkeepers, bill payers and negotiators of the family!

➢ Pursue financial education.

➢ It is essential to build relationships with financial professionals.

✍ **Make a date to go speak with your banker.**

Write specific questions to ask here. ✍

_____

_____

_____

_____

✍ **Register for a FREE financial seminar.**

Record the notes here. ✍

Topics Discussed:

_____

_____

_____

_____

Key Points from the seminar:

_____

_____

_____

_____

_____

_____

How did the seminar help you in your financial journey?

_____

_____

_____

_____

_____

_____

_____

_____

13

What do I DO now?
Taking Financial Responsibility!

The path to financial freedom is a personal one. We must see, believe, and do something in order to make a change in our financial lives. The path to financial freedom is one where we must first define what it means to us as an individual (discovering your "why"). We must explore the path that leads to how we really feel about money (what I believe), the path that propels us to get a realistic picture of where we stand in relations to money (our expense account) and the path that propels us to do something (savings and investing).

So, to recap the previous chapters, let us focus on a few simple steps. For the sake of this book, let us keep our focus **Practical**, **Relevant** and **Real**. The following pages are part of a simple plan that I discuss with my clients. It works for those who are willing to take the simple steps.

See, Believe & DO... in order to make a change in your financial life.

---

1. Discuss how you feel about money/what you were told.

Write down all the phrases you have heard over the years. Cross out those that you do not believe and highlight those you do believe.

_____   _____

_____   _____

_____   _____

_____   _____

_____   _____

_____   _____

_____   _____

_____   _____

_____   _____

2. Do a real snapshot of where you are financially (complete an Expense Account Sheet).

Income (what's coming in)		Expenses (what's going out)		Balance (what's left)
	-		=	$
	-		=	
	-		=	
	-		=	
	-		=	
	-		=	
	-		=	
	-		=	
	-		=	
	-		=	
	-		=	
	-		=	
	-		=	

3. Let's discuss why you want more money (what does financial freedom mean to YOU):

A. _____

_____

B. _____

_____

C. _____

_____

4. Let's pull all 3 credit reports:

www.annualcreditreport.com

File the reports in a binder; highlight your debts. Remember to pay off your debts, one by one each month.

Credit Report Agency	Date Pulled:
_____ **Experian** _____	_____
_____ **Equifax** _____	_____
_____ **Transunion** _____	_____

5. Let's discuss a savings plan.

***Exercise:**

A. Come up with realistic ways to save money.

B. Decide on a reasonable amount of money you wish to save each month, each week, etc.

C. Open a **SEPARATE** savings account.

D. Ask a responsible person to hold you accountable to the amount of money you choose to save. Responsible person *can be a friend or a banker.*

E. Use some of the extra money in the separate savings account to pay outstanding debts or fund your dream (once you have saved your goal amount).

F. Review your progress regularly.

Now that you have a few action steps, I ask you for the last time...

Girl, WHAT you Gonna DO with YOUR money?

Key Points:

- ➤ The path to financial freedom is personal.

- ➤ Challenge your personal beliefs about money and finance.

- ➤ We must explore the paths that leads us to how we really feel about money.

- ➤ We must have a plan... and FOLLOW it!

14

The Truth and Nothing but the Truth

There is no magic formula and there is nothing that makes me more special than the next person. It is as simple as allowing yourself to dream (see), believing in yourself (believe) and taking action (do). Adding a combination of self-discipline and what I call "delayed gratification", brought me to the place I am at today. A place where I work because I love to do what I do, not because I have to!

It was not always easy starting out. My adult life started early as a young wife and mother who had to readjust her life to raise a family. Having enough money was always a challenge.

I know television often gets a bad reputation, and rightfully so, with all the negativities being played every day. However, it was because of television that I was able to see a different type of life. I was able to see that there were lifestyles quite different than mine. Television propelled me to dream and dream big! Television is where I went to see rich people act out their lives, which allowed me to discover that there was more to living than what I was born into.

Due to my inquisitiveness, I always had a love for knowing HOW money moved and worked in our society. So, I took the time to read books, articles, pamphlets and whatever I could get my hands on, to educate myself about money and how to use it. I learned early that the examples that I grew up with were just mere groundwork and that I needed to educate myself in another way if I wanted to achieve the goals, I had set for myself. I learned early that if I ever wanted to live like the people on TV, I HAD to educate myself.

As a young woman, I started with a savings account and then loosely purchased banking products such as CD's. I became addicted to life insurance because my children were young at the time and I feared leaving them with nothing. Those large policies were very appropriate for my family during the early stages since we did not have any assets to leave our children back then. Today our investment focus has shifted however the focus is the same.

Security

Security was also important to me. I never wanted to not have or run out of anything. Leaving home to start a family at the age of 19 required me to learn quickly about the value of money. I could not concentrate on what I was not taught, I had to go into survival mode. However, there were good nuggets that I picked up along the way, like writing bills down on paper, making sure I stuck to a budget, etc. (Remember, learning how to write out my bills was a skill that I learned from peeping in my grandmother's spiral notebook on the kitchen table ☺; but the principles of saving money were never actually discussed with me.)

And buying household products in bulk was a skill that I learned from my mother. That life skill lessened my trips to the market and helped me keep more money in my pocket. Pre-planning helped me to save, even as a young woman all those years ago. Pre-planning is something that I do today. I never want to be unprepared.

Savings

I did not mention this before but, another skill I developed was paying my living expenses in advance. This relieved some financial anxiety. When I received a lump sum of cash (i.e., a tax refund check), I saved a small portion and then paid my expenses six months in advance. Instead of spending money on new cars, furniture, or clothes, like many of my friends did, I paid my bills! This allowed me to have some sense of security and freedom as well as eliminate stress about having to pay a living expense.

Let me warn you: I was talked about, ridiculed, and joked by many of my friends for driving an older model car and not spending my money as they did. However, when the month of April came and they were struggling to pay rent, my rent and utilities were paid. You see, this is what I mean by "delayed gratification." It is simply doing what you must do now so you can do what you want to later. And because I knew my dreams were bigger than my current situation (at that time), I chose to delay my spending until... well, NOW!

NOW I can buy whatever I desire! And guess what? I STILL buy sensibly (ask my closest friends)!

Bottom line: I was trying to get to where Kay Chancellor on *The Young and the Restless* was, so I did not have time to spend all my money. I am still striving today to get to Kay Chancellor's status. My focus today is still the same... Financial Freedom!

Key Points:

➤ Practicing self-discipline and delayed gratification is essential to the path financial freedom!

➤ Paying some expenses in advance may decrease some financial anxiety.

➤ Remember financial freedom requires us to see, believe and do!

What about TODAY?

My husband and I STILL allow ourselves to dream. We continue to dream pass our upbringing. We continue to challenge our beliefs and what we were taught and not taught about money. We make a point to educate ourselves on money matters for our lives. We have worked together for years to save and build our cash flow so that we can now live our dream life. The life that is important to us! Now there are several pieces that I have left out that could not be captured in this one book, so you must buy the next book in the series to find that out. However, what I WILL tell you is, we disciplined ourselves we followed a few practical principles and life is SWEET!

It is my hope that this book helps to educate and stimulate change in some, push others to their financial destiny and bring hope to ALL. If you learn nothing else from this book, I want to impress upon you that I am an everyday person, living my everyday life. And if I can do it, so can YOU!

Peace & Blessings,

Ti'Juana A. Gholson

Owner and Founder of TAG Consulting, LLC & L.I.P.S.™ (Ladies Impacting Professional Systems)

122 Girl WHAT!

About the Author

Ti'Juana A. Gholson, Speaker/Author/Coach, a member of The Maximized Life Coaching and Mentoring Team, is a Demonstrational Life & Business Coach specializing in program development, strategic planning and business structuring. As a serial entrepreneur, Ti'Juana provides EVERYDAY mentorship and coaching to small business owners and contract professionals through her company TAG Consulting.

She is also the founder of a business network called L.I.P.S.™ (Ladies Impacting Professional Systems), where she conducts monthly meetups with a group of women business owners offering support and providing a safe place to discuss business related concerns as they mastermind new business ventures and ideas.

Ti'Juana is the wife of Lawrence A. Gholson, II, the author of Mind on my Money (the male version of this book), You Factor and *Writers Readers Runners: Assembling & Establishing an Influential Winning Team* which, she patterns her practice after. She is a loving mother and the coolest NaNa of adorable grandboys. She has a master's degree in Marriage and Family Counseling and certification in Life Coaching.

Ti'Juana is a self-starter who strives to remain **Relevant**, **Relatable** and **Real**. She enjoys sharing her life story as well as encouraging others, especially women, that if SHE can be successful so can YOU!

Ti'Juana lives by the motto "Maximize YOUR Life" and she strives to *live her life on purpose with NO apologies and NO regrets*!